CHLOROSIS

DERRICK MUND

MICHAEL FLATT

the operating system print//document
CHLOROSIS

ISBN: 978-1-946031-27-3
Library of Congress Control Number: 2018948544
copyright © 2018 by Michael Flatt and Derrick Mund
edited and designed by Lynne DeSilva-Johnson

is released under a Creative Commons CC-BY-NC-ND (Attribution, Non Commercial, No Derivatives) License: its reproduction is encouraged for those who otherwise could not afford its purchase in the case of academic, personal, and other creative usage from which no profit will accrue.

Complete rules and restrictions are available at:
http://creativecommons.org/licenses/by-nc-nd/3.0/

For additional questions regarding reproduction, quotation, or to request a pdf for review contact operator@theoperatingsystem.org

This text was set in Science Fair, Gill Sans, Minion, Franchise, and OCR-A Standard.

Books from The Operating System are distributed to the trade by SPD/Small Press Distribution, and via Ingram, with production by Spencer Printing, in Honesdale, PA, in the USA.

Cover features "Ambiguity in the Face of the Cause," [thread on vintage needlepoint, 2016] by Suchitra Mattai. For more on the artist visit: http://www.suchitramattai.com

The operating system is a member of the Radical Open Access Collective, a community of scholar-led, not-for-profit presses, journals and other open access projects. Now consisting of 40 members, we promote a progressive vision for open publishing in the humanities and social sciences. Learn more at: http://radicaloa.disruptivemedia.org.uk/about/

Your donation makes our publications, platform and programs possible! We <3 You.
bit.ly/growtheoperatingsystem

the operating system
141 Spencer Street #203
Brooklyn, NY 11205
www.theoperatingsystem.org
operator@theoperatingsystem.org

CHLOROSIS

ACKNOWLEDGMENTS

Excerpts from *Chlorosis* have previously appeared in
Sink Review, Sleepingfish, and *Timber Review.*

"The Poetics of Chlorosis" and "The Poetics of Catastrophe"
were presented at the 2018 Northeast
Modern Language Association conference,
on the panel, "Tracing the Boundaries of Ecopoetic Criticism In Situ."

CONTENTS

Chlorosis - 7

The Poetics of *Chlorosis* - 81
The Poetics of Catastrophe - 84
Poetics and Process Q&A - 88
About the Authors - 97
About the Artist: Suchitra Mattai - 98

field-dressed is the morning each morning. set alive in the middle of those material abrasions we hear as traffic. maybe milk is the way we manage a fire and maybe that's why our eyes are red and pour sour with impetus. if there is a horse to be broken let it be my memory of being a broken horse wild to be broken again.

let the best thing better lest the worst thing worsen. you're in the hazy foreground of each green image. I'm saying I want to be stuck in traffic with you when you feel the dirty and young and the dying disdain of tenderness. if only for the sake of this tincture. if only for the scent of it. we'll identify the sun as such and circle it in bricksand.

my want is to care about the ways I want to care about soil ph levels. to take off your samizdat scruff and hush my nothing in the hush of a collective nothing. our mutual empties to cozy over while you are marbled with coffee grounds and diapers and acetaminophen. our choices, imping toward stasis: to be young and express a chair doing most of the talking. would you believe the heath is more beside you than this?

"I am not utterly uninterested in humans." but just how into the over-codified ideal of vibrancy am I? I mean, I'll perform a network analysis of windblown collectivities of street trash, because if the sun hadn't glinted on this mass of miscellany, I might not have stopped, pulled out my glowing architecture and captured the assemblage. I am fully aware of my materialism, but the fact that I own it does not negate it. I realize it requires "buying ever-increasing numbers of products purchased in ever-shortening cycles." but I think the more objects I touch, the less force they exert upon me, until their desperation to exert force moves them to form the coherent waves we find softly pressing us into the sand. each soliton inertly decodes our composition, the composition of our desires. do we know the tide doesn't recede by choice? again, this constitutes an objective passivity to our active subject-ness. do we qualify as active? any more so than the kinked ping-pong ball or the ripped highway tire or the lead paint chip or the squeaking floor joist or the frozen asteroid, which each move and are moved in the matter flow? one might say this movement constitutes a form of autopoesis in which the proto-actant approximates the activity of the actant. the thing-power of the gunpowder residue sampler inscribes in the thing something resembling the will of the spirit, equally unknown, unproven, and yet expounded upon for centuries thanks to our centering of the subject in our onto-poetics. on the ethical radar screen, the I is our god, and no amount of semiotic swerve will pull it from its orphaned royal throne. it will take an impossible kinship of all things. a sudden mineralization of idea into concept into being. non-identity holds sway over qualitative singularities, over the mobile set lacking a fossilized spirit. our faint gestures toward some hedonistic self-denial, the communes we never form, are killing us in this fugitive dimension.

a common anomaly, or some shitbird culture?

mining for white noise, I'll show you my road rash cartilage. I'll ask you into a game of dark darts—which is just darts in the dark. we're not here to read the sea within the sea.

we spill spit from our cheeks and lips when we fall in the white stone shit ditch. we wake up little by little by the shit we wake littled by.

do you wake up in yards after a whiteout night on the tracks? if so, how is your sheepskin blanket so bloodlessly white?

the way I dance is a gutter; all lash and backboned cherry muddle realized as my arms are reborn in the depths of this ocean this skeletal mass this cry for the grey country bland with trees.

not just grey, not just brown, not just white. just bored in a plastic tub. can't you find me diminishing? not less funny but just waiting.

both of us trying to avoid that point at which you only eat things you can eat with spoons. biological ontology is the atomization and proliferation of a self still constituted as singular.

attractive or repellent is the self in the tire change shop where the Sears used to be but now there's a Kohl's. I think this is where the Sears used to be. I know it's a tire shop. I just think it used to be a Sears-brand tire shop.

we found each tree in an outline of the riot squad talking piss in the barracks.

we found each storm drain; a cover song of the earth smeared rotten with oceans.

we found our secret cleft-lipped chants bobbing in that various sea.

why not put a corkscrew through the back of my savings? are you ready to give up on sacrifice as a means to empty our faucets? love it or leave, the you is my god, so tell it to my mercury levels at their emptiest limp. tell it to the shallow wisp of streetlamp lingering in the hall. there are questions I'm only now thinking to ask: how did my mother know not to baptize me? how do we dodge these sanguine optics?

I think you're a little too down for a drink; listen

if I were making a composite of the world's most awful lover, I think I'd include your lymph nodes and my ghost-limb second set of molars.

because whose genitals are to blame whose genitals years later when we're both green-sick breathing the half-dead air of the half-dead mammoths we are.

I tend to you like dust brushed from a dear friend

's shoulder after they've passed out

and been ashed on.

the junkyard car-tree silhouette a ziggurat of late capital. isolated economies of third-world trash-picking are the secret fantasies of NSA threesome ads on Craigslist. this barely interrupted pleasure with no visible consequence betrays the source of our chemical and affective toxicity. some link between the image of the sleeping woman in men's lyric poetry and the image of animals landfill-grazing. a means to an end user agreement. the pastoral beauty into which we gel subjectivities in lyricism runs parallel to an erotic fixation upon a soft-focus ideal of the feminine. the digital processing of color makes for a chemical recomposition of lust that resists decomposition. the language is pressurized beneath a dense pseudo-bleu ciel which has grown as human as the unfolding metropoli, the corrugated-steel-and-plastic slums bridging Cape Town and Caracas. the oil-soaked seagull of the Gulf Coast doesn't shock enough to cause more than a flinch. it is a matter of course, and as such is interpolated into the New Organic, an alloy of geobodily affect and neuroatmospheric chemistry.

your breathing in my sleep

is a scattered negative reflection

of an apology

or

stop

the metaphor isn't forgetting

so much as it is not.

a tape recorder
caught in your slow-talking fuckblur
picking up the sound of its own winding
sleaze in this dubious tryst.

declension in all its furious harmonies

that siren of being just

done

call me floss-flushed and denuded.

can me carrion fidgeting peptides.

stow me in the backseat under a tarp sliced up with your jingles.

in every sense of the word in the blank of the impossible you, nothing left but moisturizer, an enormous plaid scarf, and a backpack with your parents' address on the tag.

it's raining green and it's all over your face but you're too drunk to feel it. can you hear the way out? is space and silence the opposite of skin-mixing salted knells? go ahead. we already know your jaundiced roar. we already know we were born to be incubated. we already know we're the children that don't live long enough to be named.

this lugubrious fist crowns against the unrest of a crested sun

in its worn-out gums

beaten like a rug

is Mothra on any Saturday afternoon

I say "I" after I think the two of us will be gutted

        the mothlike clouds of your midwest placing

        a set of radial spokes in place;

        I say "then what lakeless non-nation have we infested with our floundering?"

I woke up to the sound of chickens, thinking I was dead.

it was a sound that did not make sense.

it was a sound and I had not heard for a very long time.

the mosquito haze
breaks its amber corona
against your texted nudes
which are of course
always sunsets

we are rutting on our helplessness riled up

on grayness mating with itself, making such gray noises we notice the worthlessness of words, the wordlessness of worth.

between organic indifference and gilded action, the terrain of this motel roof will be our repeated argument.

too busy trying to redraw reality to see what reaching the conclusion of
an unobserved solstice engenders.

and still the breathless reaction to a turn is

still

the breathless reaction to a turn.

like the earth keeps on

like a place

lacking its geography

because it does not have a place,

    a burrowed gravitational compression-ore gelatinous center to
    its spherical compass

a tactic

depends on time

it is always on watch

for a consideration of place

it was easy to be near me again
like an old thing without its old badness

a tire sale in a rebirthed bad part of a now differently bad part of town it'll smell and feel the same and the memories of older televisions will occupy the desert it eclipses and mountains with gagged images and scents of how terrible it is to always be alive in a skin you can only shed every seven years or so.

but there is no goodness in old things
only the comfort of "oh, you've got _____ eyes."

city declared indefinite.

cloud presented a solution to the sun.

plant whispered when watered.

rhubarb patch boiled down and braided.

I had earlier in adulthood this suit but

it threw off a texture proven too bronchial.

the myth of stasis, an LED grid sparking behind the printed words, glitch-funnels into our ears. whether we still hover near the homeostatic is irrelevant in the midst of this upstate tick epidemic. Lyme Disease is Lyme Disease is us stuck in a house out in the woods like we wanted it. when ponds acquire the salinity of body fluid, all manner of *objets* learn how to float. no amount of tidal flushing will rinse that flow, nor should it. the oscillations of predator-prey populations unhinge the mirrored septic-flesh state of faith, as faith is the science of belief. the science of the skeptic in a proven geospatial whatever. " the current popular model is a descriptive error." ok, but does the gemstone tremble at the miner's approach, or has the negative entropy inherent to its extraction made it fearless? "stasis does not appear to be, for any component of the universe, a very permanent phenomenon." but when a thermodynamic flow breaks like a bottle on a curb and wipes out our species, who is to say this isn't a kind of ideological semaphoric projection? there remains the positive entropy of human embrace, the predictable ebbs and flows of sensory pleasure. the heat exchanged in language is now diffuse, but you're right, it would be cold to call these simply resource inputs.

we are untouched. we slip our hands into the sand of a frozen beach. the land impedes our passage to the wood's watering sound. the soil is soldered to our bloodlet sense of what it is to be a being in the presence of two bodies at rest. I have crossed the street and I know what it is to have been destroyed by crossing the street. all but your voice is noise on which my torso glides. I was carried to the shoulder without knowing my carriers would blink away the glare but not its manic inversion of speech. this version reaches the sand which was as cool on your scalp as an inherited crown. the chandelier gleaned no more in the twilight than the body half-submerged in the creekbed.

so, it wasn't all great.

in the backyard you build an effigy for all those small bits of birds in some lake where we used to lick small tufts of grass under the telephone wire where I love you is a wonderful expression of the way we mop around the space that occupies the conversations we have. the grey country white with coniferous trees blank and omaha in their sway against against against nonchalance out on the pavement the lamina moon scrapes rings from the posies under the blooming squelch of sun.

I like the way daisies seem dirty off the highway 90-some miles outside of the phrase of a town I keep forgetting I like the way this awkward globalism offers an apology of I guess so yeah all this imaginary pornography is hilarious super hilarious but it's making me sick like how the letters are just blocked out before sound it's making me like the barely recalled basement-muffled voices with a nightstand way of thinking each way you blushed was made up of the blanks found in the compost.

this way I get all song of winter
(and say)

I love your plucked-
eyebrow way
of going about things

is you to I contingent
on the way a tree bends
in what we make of wind
or the way we've
made it bend,
a tree tripping on top of itself

is this bend
what we make
so oxbow
so thorned

but flood, should
you shake these
trees to orgasm

I'll hold my tongue
while I scrub your body
with whatever
you find yourself lugging
around inside of me

but
instead
i
think
of
this
cloud
file
like
a
receiver

still
and
outside
of
the
infected
and

infected
and
outside
of
the
still

or something extinct
in that early bird diner
and its patient waitresses
or my incipience
in the snow
where a stranger stopped the mountain
from moving for a geologic moment of interest

we should have worked
tectonics
where
a
berm
has
occluded
my
memory

we breathe fog into the machine fog

change our mood

another rotted futurity of false
positive epiphanies

is the gloveless local asking
to shovel
my front walk

no, just take something
jesus, for yourself

I am mostly a subaudible tightening of shoulder tendons
waiting indefinitely on something indefinite

look at me taking sound for granted the way my mouth makes rust look like little pockets of air in the sand like I gather dust in your bedroom like our mouths might fill with silt if we sit with our mouths opened on this dune long enough.

listen.

this erosion
is talking sweet to you.

this sort of ending finds me standing at the local frozen margarita stand,

watching a buddy watch the social sport of being shitty in public, thinking

of thirteen ways to slam his dick in this screen door

of a blackbird

but when we walked you made a wake beside me in a burning pile of leftover kinks

on the ridge ripe with leftover sentiment

if we talk about the buried

we can, maybe,

piss on some flowers

along the way

while they

wake and smile

with the dread of the clamoring detail

of the wakened day

can you make this moment
more or less slivered?

we can meet, yes, but,
have you ever seen how great
I am at being dismissive?

what if instead of pursuing procession we track a greater sense of proprioception, this being the attempted boundary of commodified faux-co-op-shopping liberalism, in which we self-implicate in the proliferation of endless reproduction, a cat o' nine flagellation. but we might remove those blinders to find that the sense of balance, or a sharpened sensitivity to imbalance, shifts our affective heft, might demystify our relationship to the "perplexed machine," which is surely a sexual one, surely a collapsing romance. and so we are of course surrounded by it. of course there is no division between the natural space and the human space. to extract value from all beings and all things until the link between being and thing crags and shifts subductively is to populate our hearts with the pelican decayed sufficiently to reveal a belly full of trash. but the sentimental horror of such an image is useless unless the PTSD symptoms of climate scientists cross-pollinates with the heat in New Dehli, which we are told is "literally unbearable ... especially for the poor."

to hear within the immense night
still more immense without

the radioactive passerine regurgitations
swank with woe

I've worn myself out on our disgust

and in the incidental curvature
of this conversion
how much
can we sustain

and tell a heart something
without some backing vox
as the bridge builds

and our one-leaf eyes are still broken

each movement another earthly tradition
slung from a trebuchet

and the industrial midwest
enters the uncanny valley of
"is he serious about that flag magnet?"

read this desperate grift
as a chancy appellative

the serrated edge is geological;
a single-celled sea
is the seamonkey house
you die in is still the still earth

the difference precedes and postdates
without difference
this wilderness you still die in
and nothing within us is the way we waver
like a disobedient animal
staggered and hoping for someone
to be so unwaveringly open

that we age
like minerals
ored from the earth
in countries
we couldn't give a shit about
stars that come and go
in the last and first light of
stars they come out slow
and they come
in the first and last light of a blaze

and they sit down

and they are still
slow lights

I can't
say I get
coral

but coral's past caring
what I get

you thought there was
a word for that
color
for two stars growing
closer together
the riff becoming
densely grained
with wear

or circular with elegy
I if I close
each yellow word
except my eyes
what I see
is livid with little yellow nights

and in an afternoon
you thought there was a word for a color
for two stars growing
closer together

their riff becoming
densely grained
as dense with wear
as with circular elegy

and if I close
each yellow word
I don't see the sun

because I'm not trying to see the sun

this laurel

this ocean

this pivot of violet

and unfit lipstick

is can I put my skin on

what the air wears

spooky action at a contingent

is if this be error

is it me

or the enormous emoting

of a giant gong

but it won't make much difference as long as all apologies are still sick out on the lawn getting used to this blood buzz. I'm sorry, I've just been busy with quotable dust is a house you may remember the plane that crashed into a house near the airport and killed forty-nine people in the plane and one in the house.

yeah, I get it;

your life is hilarious with want

in the desert
opposition is easy

what we posit is not
our varied nature;
an absent violence
is the sea we bend toward

still and waking for that which we lack
from which to emerge

I am the moment I long for still
in the moment I was longing

at this point a moment is still what
we're driving for, still trajectory
to remove ourselves from stasis

to put an office in the middle of an art gallery is to sob
and then apologize

the getaway is indifference
to the idea of you
sitting in a car
in this heat

this absentee obscenity standing in
for the stand-in sun saves each wild breath
each dragnet melody
bent across the floor
the leaden lake we left so green,

trucks out the formerest of my
bloodmissive sighs
in malleable dust
we can each puddle about
our respective mud huts but what
you trust isn't what you puddle

No cloud or dumpster
has ever looked real and
neither has your herring-bone mask
or any part of me below the waist.

each finger-smudge drawing

wrote out its water-logged memory

played this that this there

rendered

one charm incensed

distracted

so neither food

nor sleep

could cover my eyes

but tossed,

bed-lain

nightly

tricks, spit, penalties

ask again

but more drifted

I am as much its root structure as its branches, blight, and drone. its mechanisms silence when I do. when I whir, they whir. I will be a dried-up fire stirring coals for the early afternoon spring humid sky. I am as much a function of the forest as the forest is a function of me. when I am alone in the desert the forest surrounds me. when I am in a dense but empty sky I am in the endless forest. there is such a thing as bright-dark absence. think this forest moon clothed in its endless conspiring. what might be called the expanding notion of an expanding modality as a universe in the act of its expansion as a single piano key panging away is something contained. dirt clouded and alive in the sense that it moves. in geologic terms, whenever I walk I spin in a perpetual center, the still and rhythmic movement of the endless forest floor. unwound through time into sediment, just I will be filled with grease and smoldering beaches.

I want to be able to call

this navigable space

protection

and believe it

the problem with a box

is you can sell it

with a security-camera view of the mountains' tracts

with the last recorded portion of our voice

we were an injurious phrase
born within a structure
only to be disclosed by its debris
and the soft words our world became blight with a methane burp
a mute lingual resin
a breath with no-
thing beneath it

the slow loss of the Maldives
the slow loss of mobility

more traceable in arthritis

waiting on some sense of blank while
the corner divides itself in three

in a passed-out-in city park

observing the loss of surface

through pinpoint punctures

blanketing the gravel creek

creeping in pink-sequined

contortionist distortions

atop the orange/blue contrast orations

every few feet

a bird in the face

of a small

and terrified kid

and no matter how Dionysian your hum

I will still call it a cop-out

who will blink first? you

or the ground

rank with blank

and moss or that door

locked

as you left

burdened with ideas

this earth

bent toward a yellowed point

of an orbiting satellite

a colorless rhythm in the
cone of headlight rippling along

an unseasonable
narrow of bodies

the kindness of digging

to say goodbye

the wind-dimpled terrain of minor tributaries

feeding a sulfurous creek

we get so gash

it hushes the buzz we keep being

the children's ears
rattle a little form of echo

like that laurel

thought it could
clap open song

watching this train
slowly burn the tracks

and leave them writhing in their own light

to be just like being
ok is equally

as ok as it is not to be clotting
is a way to cauterize being in photos

where the problem
isn't who's keeping

or unsheathing the knife but
how the knife was made

In a sink with its basin of stars
I get chatty in the drone
(riled up on yerba mate
and a hangover
something about fucking)

in the difference
between a wheel
and a turnstile
blades of linoleum bloom.

words say everything I love

if you need me
I'll be acting the ocean

look: I have no idea about all my mouths
overgrown with irises

the mumbled halogens
touch a tumescent belly

a body or a determined and repeated motion
like geraniums being stitched to cubicle glass
with the calmness of the pale yellow air

a place begins to
lack its geography

as it loses its consideration for time

meanwhile, in the weird west, we gather in a park where the moths become a way to say, "I'm waiting for the catastrophe as quietly as I can."

we end at the sea

for now its sunfish

don't eat the half moon

the half moon eats the parasites
off the sunfish as do the gulls
floating on the kelp of these seaweed rafts
rotting and

when I vomit you out

      I dazzle the light

beneathem

this is double

no, this is double
is finding where all the ants are
coming from.
is it all the spilt honey?
there is a mole
an informant
a rat
licking up all
the ants
gathering honey
off my abdomen

in this way my belly button
is a flower
but not an orchid
god I hope it's not an orchid
as I'm frightened by hummingbirds
anywhere

just thought you should know
I've been in Hong Kong in my mind
all this whole time

it's filthy
the way we look at each star
with nostalgia for a summer camp

and that time before we knew
how our indelicate eyes would go

despite the woods left out
in the woods I thought your voice was sweet
like an apartment
promises

to be a burden
I woke up this morning
fully clothed
clutching a can of bear spray

still half-dreaming of closing down one
kidney and then the other
a few years later

we spend most of our time
within things made
during the acid shift
locked in bystander
syndrome dreams

posies seem the ideal
way to get wobbly
in the shutter-
orange winced-up night
with its plastic bag windows

Occasionally, the most satisfying thing is to administrate a funeral.

to come to
in the looming
blue shame
of ionic dispersal

and then realize
everything is done
and is boring

a flowering dirt
gilded
in the gross
cross section of morning

semblance
waved from a passing window
frames memory
of a lamplight
or living for the supermarket
blues to come rolling on

an instant in a space
surrounding a belly river
an amaryllis patch pawing from its bank

dozing in the inflorescence
a refrain
reverberates to its moss womb

THE POETICS OF
CHLOROSIS

This project began fairly organically. We had worked together here and there throughout grad school and had a familiarity with each other's work. So the project began as a typical writer-to-writer correspondence about aesthetics, our respective stylistic tendencies, giving each other encouragement and letting one another know when something we'd written was a bit much, kind of boring, or too obscure. The conversations then turned to content. We quickly realized that our two major themes were romantic relationships and urban ecology, and we decided to start working together on a project based on these themes.

To begin, we did what many collaborators these days do. We opened a shared Google Doc and started cramming it with text. One of the key rules to our process, which took control of the work away from any one author, was our freedom to cut and add as we wished. Anything could be removed. Anything could be added. This is a process we would consider a (soma)tic exercise. The poet CA Conrad writes, "The word Soma is derived from the Sanskrit and Indo-European tongues meaning 'to press and be newly born.' Our idea for a (soma)tic poetics is a poetry which investigates that seemingly infinite space between body and spirit by using nearly any possible THING around or of the body to channel the body out and/or in toward spirit with deliberate and sustained concentration."

Through *Chlorosis*, we explored the nature of writing as a giving up or giving away of intentionality. The "THING" we each used, in addition to the typical notebook, pen, and word-processing software, was the other person, that being whose own lived experience, their daily interactions with other things and beings, was allowed into our creative ecosystem, like an invited invasive species. Through this form of collaboration—in which one's own artistic output is perpetually modified by the presence and will of another person—we hoped for something "newly born" to emerge.

We've seen what we think are three newly born, or dialectical, elements produced by our collaboration. First, as the work was continually manipulated between countless exchanges, edits, and rewrites, a new speaker emerged, whose voice neither of us can claim as his own. We can no longer identify much of the work in *Chlorosis* as having been written by either of us. There are of course pages over which one of us would say we had more of an influence, just as there are pages clearly inflected by the other's language. But on the whole, it feels as though this text was written by someone else. Reading from the text is a very odd experience, knowing that we've each had a definite hand in crafting the language, but seeing so little of our own language in it. Our process was a means for this dialectic to reveal itself.

The speaker of these poems is transient, at times grounded in the geographic realities we have experienced in Denver, Buffalo, Syracuse, Detroit, Aspen, Browning, Baab, Kalispell, Portland, and Coeur D'alene. At many points, however, the geography is indistinct, a phantasmagorical pastiche of images of ecological blight taken from American urban landscapes as well as those encroached upon by development and other human influence. The indefinite site of definite decay, which we understand as a metonymic representation of the more general ecological collapse, slowly spread through the manuscript and became the dominant theme, which lead to giving our book the name of a leaf disease whose name translates as "greensickness."

The third object to emerge within this space is an undefined lyrical object, an unidentified "you." The connections between speakers, objects, and second person characters is paratactical at its base. We both may have originally had specific "you"s in mind but as the work evolved, grew, was born into itself, the "you" became an apparition. There's an amnesiac quality to the text, in which the you is at once detailed enough to leave concrete evidence like "a backpack with your parents' name on the tag" but sufficiently undefined to allow the "you" to refer to objects, events, or ecology itself. While writing, we allowed ourselves to forget our intentions and voices, and we tried to create something unrooted.

Stylistically, *Chlorosis* toggles between prose poems that have an expository, almost essayistic tone and image- and sound-driven, lyrical verse. This formal approach allowed for the juxtaposition of several modes of engagement between syntactic experimentation, detailed imagery, pointed observations, unquoted everyday speech, and echolalic sound-play. Through a kind of perversion of the lyric, these poems seek to address a fundamental poetic question: to what extent is communication possible? In a poetic work focusing on decay as subject matter, a goal of ours was to bring the lyric to a point of decay by stripping away representation and syntactic meaning-making. To quote poet and essayist Elisa Gabbert, "The best perfumes are completely abstract," which is to say, they don't smell like any one thing in a representative way. As any reader of Gertrude Stein can tell you, language can do this too, and there's a kinship between the semiotic dissection of language and the slow violence taking place in our cities, towns, and natural spaces. The result of this lyrical decay recalls the "uncertainties" of Keats' negative capability, the comfort of the writer and reader in communicating outside of conventional logic. Chlorosis embraces decay as something new, even as the earth threatens to move on without us.

THE POETICS OF
CATASTROPHE

The focus of this brief essay will be to introduce the notion of the Poetics of Catastrophe, a poetics that we certainly would not claim to have founded, but one in which we see ourselves participating. We will distinguish this poetics from the simple description of catastrophe found in many ecopoetic texts and from the sentimental serving up of contrast between the components of a false binary, a culture halved between pastoral representations of nature, a place of sanctuary and peace, and grotesque treatments of man-made conditions of waste. We will outline an understanding of our material condition as described by Bruno Latour and Jane Bennett, and discuss poetry's particular stake in materiality. Lastly, we will argue for poetry as an ideal site for the generation of speculative theory, of writing-as-opening.

In an essay entitled "Wastepickers and the Seduction of the Ecopoetical Image," Ted Mathys describes what he calls the "perception hypothesis," which presumes that the use of so-called experimental poetic practices such as associative logic, juxtaposition, and metaphor, as outlined in Marcella Durand's essay "The Ecology of Poetry," can intuitively alter the way the reader sees the world. In this essay, Durand admires Juliana Spahr's willingness to place bulldozers in proximity to birds, thereby polluting what might be called the nature-walk sensibility of early ecopoetry. The hoped-for result of this supposed crossing of boundaries is "increased perception, and increased change." Mathys observes that the perception hypothesis presumes a "wilderness" that is separate and apart from human influence, upon which humans may sometimes infringe, but which is at its heart untouched by human hands. In what has come to be known as the age of the sixth mass extinction, we know that we need not have even seen a species in order to wipe it from the earth. There is no earthly territory that stands outside of human influence, and thus, the juxtaposition of natural purity and man-made profanity assumes a false binary. Mathys proposes a poetics of accumulation that deploys images of conglomeration and accretion to help readers understand the global economics of waste streams and the informal economy of wastepickers in the developing world, who make a living sorting and carrying our plastic bottles that will eventually be made into Chinese fiber-optic cable. He writes, "We can't see the informal economy unless we are trained to see iteratively, to see in process and progression." Mathys here advocates for poetry that mimetically reproduces and therefore renders visible the hidden economies of global capital.

The Poetics of Catastrophe functions differently. Rather than playing the role of ideological documentary, which would hope to enact change by making the reader familiar with the logic of exploitation—a worthwhile enterprise meaningfully undertaken by such poets as Mark Nowak, Daniel Borzutsky, and others—the Poetics of Catastrophe is marked by the attempt to innovate new modes of intellectual engagement, often through a collage of disciplinary approaches. Recognizable in the work of Mei-Mei Berssengbrugge, CA Conrad, Judith Goldman, and angela rawlings, among others, we see this approach making use of the generic and intellectual flexibility of contemporary poetry to experiment with the intermixing of modes of inquiry, breaking down a centuries-old division of science, social science, and the humanities.

The need for such a breakdown has been articulated by the social scientist Bruno Latour in his 1991 book, *We Have Never Been Modern*. "Our intellectual life is out of kilter," Latour writes. "In the eyes of our critics, the ozone hole above our heads, the moral law in our hearts, the autonomous text, may each be of interest, but only separately. That a delicate shuttle should have woven together the heavens, industry, texts, souls, and moral law—this remains uncanny, unthinkable, unseemly." By keeping the humanities, social sciences, and sciences isolated from one another, human intellectual activity has resulted in a variety of "hybrids," dangerous, unforeseen results of well-meaning inventions such as the aerosol spray can. The "delicate shuttle" which Latour and his colleagues proposed in the 1980s was actor-network theory, in which an extremely diverse range of things, known as actants, influence one another in powerful ways that are undetectable when we privilege human activity as the only significant activity that takes place in our reality. By identifying the network of actants at work in, to use Latour's example, ozone depletion—such as the perfluorocarbons found in aerosol spray cans, the corporations packaging and selling their products in those aerosol cans, the advertisements influencing consumers to buy them, as well as the ideologies at work that make the appeals of the advertisements effective—we can more effectively address the issue, and to do so requires a "shuttling" amongst a wide range of disciplines in order to intervene in the scientific, social, and ideological operations taking place. Contemporary poetry serves as an ideal site for radical interplays between textual disciplines, due to its eminent capaciousness—the willingness of its readers to accept hybrid genres, modulation between prose, verse, and visual art, as well as between tonal registers, specialized language, and levels of diction. The gnosticism of the lyric found in Conrad's somatics, the interlacing of historical and scientific texts with online advertising and art criticism in Judith Goldman's *Blank Mount*, the use of field recordings, and site-specific installations and photography in angela rawlings and Chris Turnbull's *The Great Canadian* all point to an experimentalism that goes beyond a diversity of linguistic approaches to embrace the sort of cross-disciplinary practice that Latour advocates. (It's also worth mentioning that the implementation of scientific language in poetry is not strictly a contemporary phenomenon, as one may find in, to name just one precursor, the nineteenth-century botanical poems of Erasmus Darwin.)

Building on Latour's actor-network theory, Jane Bennett's "vibrant materiality" seeks to dispense with accepted binaries guiding our understanding of matter. Among her goals in *Vibrant Matter* is "to dissipate the onto-theological binaries of life/matter, human/animal, will/determination, and organic/inorganic using arguments and other rhetorical means to induce in human bodies an aesthetic-affective openness to material vitality." She continues, "I want to promote . . . more attentive encounters between people-materialities and thing-materialities." We would argue that poetry has done this since its inception, as poetry is always implicitly concerned with the material by which its message is carried, that is, its medium. Before the manuscript era, when poetry was the stuff of memory, poets utilized rhyme to expand their pneumonic capacity. When poetry was first recorded, it was etched on stone shapes representative of the poem's content, as in the Greek poetry of Simmias of Rhodes, whose poems took on the shapes of an egg, an axe, and wings. When those poems were transcribed and published in the early print era, they inspired the early visual poetry page-play of George Herbert's *The Temple*. We can trace these tendencies through the twentieth century, which saw an explosion of material experimentation from the Italian Futurists to the concrete poets, the later "dirty concrete" poets, through early digital poetry, and into the present where we can see PDF poets testing the limits of what is possible with Adobe's portable document format. And of course, we have the Objectivists: Zukofsky, Niedecker, Oppen, and Williams, the latter of whom famously noted that there were "no ideas but in things." Thus it is only appropriate that poets continue to explore and demonstrate the vibrancy of matter Bennett describes.

And this is where the notion of "catastrophe" comes in. One might say the equilibrium of vibrancy has been upset by our anthropocentric hubris. The poetics of catastrophe is driven by that helplessness we feel as we witness all manner of storms of increasing intensity take place with greater frequency, as the flood waters outstrip our sandbag levees year after year, as our power lines collapse under branches that give way because they never still have their leaves when an ice storm hits, but this year they do. It is the clear urgency of our ecological crisis that drives poets to respond to it with increasingly aggressive strategies. As Latour points out, "Ever since Madame de Guermante's salon, we have known that it took a cataclysm like the Great War for intellectual culture to change its habits slightly and open its doors to the upstarts who had been beyond the pale before." Our cataclysm is not a war, or we should say, not just a war, but the combination of hybrids that have resulted in our incomparably toxic eco-political state. And thus, the Poetics of Catastrophe is a response to that toxicity, a desperate recapitulation of our intellectual cultures that hopes to reveal in its speculative theorizations and mad alchemies openings into alternative modes of thinking and being.

POETICS AND PROCESS:
A CONVERSATION WITH DERRICK MUND,
MICHAEL FLATT, AND LYNNE DESILVA-JOHNSON

Welcome! Thank you so much for taking the time to talk with us today. Can you each introduce yourself in the way that you would choose?

Hello, we're derrick mund and Michael Flatt. Mike is a PhD candidate in the SUNY Buffalo Poetics Program, a book designer and founder of Low Frequency Press. Derrick is an art events promoter and bartender. Both of us write poetry.

When did you decide you were a poet (and/or: do you feel comfortable calling yourself a poet, what other titles or affiliations do you prefer/ feel are more accurate)? In what ways, forms, and materials does your creative process manifest itself?

It's hard for us to sum up our interest in poetry with the word "poet." That implies we're most interested in getting our work published. We're just as invested in designing books, publishing the work of others, teaching poetry to students, putting readings together, etc. Creating a space to engage with language as a means of interpreting and interacting with our surroundings and unhinged landscape. Being a poet for us is really just being a member of the community, engaging in as many ways as we usefully can.

What's a "poet," anyway?

Well, machines are writing a lot of poetry these days. Mike's been pretty interested in Twitter bots for the last year or so. @tinyprotests is a good follow. As far as humans go, though, maybe a working definition of a poet would be one who tests the boundaries of what is possible with language, exposes its underlying ideologies, its concealed architectures, or places it in new and revealing medial contexts. But it's really best to keep these definitions loose and permeable. Neither of us is keen on labels.

What is the role of the poet today / what do you see as your cultural and social role (in the poetry community and beyond)? What other work are you doing in the world and how does it interface with your creative practice at this time?

As a grad student, Mike is teaching, and learning every day how to be a better teacher and thinker. Designing syllabi, compiling reading lists, working fervently to keep up with the heavy reading load he gives my students, and planning energetic, innovative lessons all help him be a better writer. As a book designer, Mike gets to see what does and doesn't transfer from manuscript to printed text, and to think about the form of the book and about letterforms.

Derrick works at a music and burlesque venue. So he's involved with a lot of different local artists outside of poetry as it's conventionally defined, which is refreshing. This is where he's found what he calls his "unidentified poets." This is a fold he instinctively gets along with. Sometimes a fellow poet is just someone you hit a vibe with who has a craft. Unidentified poets need community as much as those of us who consider ourselves "poets" in the written word sense.

The poet's role might be to help people tune into frequencies they're missing. All good art functions this way, but poetry in particular helps people see the parts of the perceptible world that their minds are ignoring, without needing to first distract you with a story. Poetry provides what other art provides, but in a more concentrated form.

How did you meet and become collaborators? What made you want to work together? How did this project, in particular, emerge and come into being?

We met in grad school and have been sharing work with each other since. Initially we wanted to work together because we saw some interesting overlaps and useful differences in our writing style. Mike had started becoming very sentence-based in his poetry with something almost "anti-lyric" in style and Derrick was onto some really strange, interesting stuff with fragments and syntactic manipulations. But we were working with a similar tonal pallet, and we shared a similar sense of humor that, while making us chuckle, acknowledges and reaffirms the bleakness of our times, economically, socially, environmentally, etc. A lot of this was motivated by the incredible rate of gentrification in Denver around 2013. So-called "development" is responsible for so much suffering and destruction. We soon began circling the idea of writing about our relationship with the Earth itself as a broken, toxic thing.

In Chlorosis *you have co-created a collection of untitled poems, engaging "with voices from the fields of ecopoetics and new materialism." Is there a specific intention or goal you had for the work? Whose voices or work were you looking to as inspiration?*

In the more essayistic passages of the text, we're mining the work of Bruno Latour, Jane Bennett, Graham Harmon, and a lot of other stuff deriving from the "process-based" philosophy of Alfred North Whitehead. The basic premise of these authors' work is a more flattened ontology that de-centers the human from our understanding of reality, and brings into consideration the ways that the friction caused in the interactions between unacknowledged entities—microbeads, perfluorocarbons, etc.—is shaping experience as much as decisions humans make. We're also trying to engage in a form of detournement on the level of the sentence, recognizing the reduction of culture to representation and responding with a mix of the abjectly absurd, the unrepresentable. At the same time, there's a futility in trying to escape the spectacle; this is the nature of detournement. That may be where the bleakness of our imagery comes from.

Talk about the process of making this work, both independently and together. Did you have this intention or develop the idea for a while? What encouraged and/or confounded this (or a book, in general) coming together? What was unexpected or surprising, if anything, about the process? How did it change or evolve?

Our process would probably be familiar to many poets who decide to collaborate these days. We opened a shared Google doc and just starting pouring stuff into it. We both work from notebooks, and anything that was worth keeping went into the Google doc. We allowed each other to edit anything that went in. We allowed ourselves to corrupt each other's poems. Usually we were trying to push it in the direction the other wanted it to go, but sometimes we wanted to throw a wrench in what the other was doing. Of course, we could always pull the wrench out, but it was a signal: "Hey, maybe don't get so scholarly here," or, "Let's lighten things up a bit," or, "I may have planted a narrative in the pages you added just to see if you can spot it." A lot of it was very playful.

I love Christopher Nealon's description of Chlorosis *as "a moving experiment in the uses of the poetic 'we' in a time of crisis." He goes on to say that as you "survey together a world in which there is no respite from the oncoming disaster, that 'we' becomes as tiny, nimble pivot for unexpected clarities and also for the testing out of tentative rhythms."*

How do you respond to this? What was your intention with the 'we'? I find that the way pronouns and the addressed "you" and "your" in the work to be very rich with myriad readings—coming into a text with two authors, the reader can vacillate from a reading that might be the authors speaking to each other, vs. a unified voice addressing the reader or a public.

We appreciate the ambiguity of the pronouns. As you're pointing out, the "we" can be read as the authors speaking together or separately from their respective relationships with a similarly ambiguous "you," which could be a loved one—lover, family member, friend—the other author, or the Earth, or all at once. There are various speakers/characters negotiating a doomed landscape. As to Nealon's "pivot," collaboration is a way of finding clarity within an otherwise ambiguous and variant narrative. The "we" also functions as the character of the chorus. As for "no respite," that was very much the feeling we were meditating on. Of course, there's a lot less respite in 2018 than there was in 2013. We'll be lucky if there isn't a coast-to-coast forest fire in five years.

How did the collaboration process work in the coordination and production of a seamless text wherein there is no obvious distinction between each of your individual voices or production? Was that the intention from the beginning?

Once we decided to collaborate beyond just exchanging work it was the intention from the onset. Once most of the text was set in place we manicured sections to our own aesthetics. We each definitely have sections that are more ours, but even those have been edited pretty heavily by the other person.

It would be strange to us to have a collaborative text with different names on different poems. Does anyone do that? Maybe it would be pretty cool. But we wanted something where our words bled together until they were often unrecognizable to us, and that's what we got.

To what extent were you working independently or together? How did you go about the editorial process in this case? Were the pieces developed collaboratively from individual texts that started in a different form? Would it be possible to see any part of the process through incremental edits in any way? It could be interesting for the audience to see how a page or pages evolved, how your voices combined, were parsed and edited to become what we see now.

Unfortunately, any record of what was what along the way was disposed of by the autosave feature on Google Docs. We mostly worked separately. Later, we got together to write for it once or twice when we were both still in Denver, and then once to give a draft of the manuscript a marathon edit.

What formal structures or other constrictive practices (if any) do you use in the creation of your work? Have certain teachers or instructive environments, or readings/writings of other creative people (poets or others) informed the way you work/write?

We mostly saw ourselves working on a spectrum between the fragment and the prose block. Some poems are lineated, others are not. In the composition phase, it was really whatever came out. But in the editing phase, we wanted there to be a tidal flow to the book's form, oscillating along that spectrum.

Whose work or presence in the world is really influencing you or your work right now? Can you talk a little bit about why?

Mei-Mei Berssenbrugge has been on Mike's mind a lot for the last few years. There's a lot of her in Chlorosis, at least in what he contributed. She embraces abstraction in a way that many poets eschew, and yet you also get an extremely grounded and tactile sense of her phenomenological connection to her surroundings. Her work can put you in a bit of a trance. For Derrick, DJ Spooky's Rhythm Science has been a strong influence. His approach to remix as a writing practice is central to the process we used for this project. Always Emily Dickinson. Her intense focus on the minutiae of language is a constant inspiration. The Heidelberg Project in Detroit amazing and constantly changing. Elisa Gabbert's work is the cat's pajamas. She has a sharp, insightful, and timeless wit.

The title, Chlorosis, comes from a leaf disease caused by lack of light, literally translated as "green sickness." Does your process of naming (poems, sections, etc) influence you and/or color your work specifically? At what point of the process did you come to this title? What kept you away from creating distinctions, titles, or sections within the text?

Choosing that the title may shaped the content a bit. Or at least lent it focus. The poet Carrie Lorig once described titles as "tupperware," and that may explain our lack of interest in them. Making a poem a neatly packaged thing, discrete from the work around it never interested us as much as making book-length projects that push the reader to interpret them as such. We almost never use titles if we can avoid it. These don't need to be read as discrete poems. The effect of one hopefully bleeds into the next, creates some friction, some unforeseen hybrids.

What does, or might, this book do (as much as what it says or contains)?

We hope the book helps people find some kinship in the feeling that the world may not want us as we are, and maybe help people realize our current strategies for enacting ecopolitical change are failing, and that we need to get more creative. Trying to alter our consumer-waste patterns is fine, but it will never be enough, and it doesn't excuse us from the work of trying to effect change on the macro level.

What would be the best possible outcome for this book? What might it do in the world, and how will its presence as an object facilitate your creative role in your community and beyond? What are your hopes for this book, and for your practice?

It will probably be useful as a source of light and heat one day. Until then, aside from perhaps acting as a small ecological intervention, we think it can function as a teaching tool for those who would like to work collaboratively, and as a method to teach remix poetry/collage language to anyone looking into the subject.

Do you plan to continue working together? What is next for each of you?

We would definitely write another book together. Maybe in a decade or so, if the atmosphere still supports human life. Mike's wrapping up the PhD program this year, so what comes next is anybody's bet. Maybe a book about the death of shopping malls? Derrick's working on a poetic play involving Cthulu, and other creation myths. Also promoting artists, writers, musicians, performers and events.

Let's talk a little bit about the role of poetics and creative community in social activism, in particular in what I call "Civil Rights 2.0," which has remained immediately present all around us. I'd be curious to hear some thoughts on the challenges we face in speaking and publishing across lines of race, age, privilege, dis/ability, class, social/cultural background, and sexuality within the community, vs. the dangers of remaining and producing in isolated "silos."

Derrick has done a lot to give a diverse range of voices a platform through his work with the Leon Reading Series in Denver, and his work with SpringGun. Mike did the same in his time at Counterpath, and does similar work with Low Frequency. Of course, this often feels difficult, especially with respect to class and socio-cultural background. We have to contend with the fact that exposure poetry is a privileged phenomenon. It's too easy to say we can only take the poetry community as it is. Mike wrote a proposal this year for a New York State Public Humanities Fellowship that would create a series of workshops geared towards workers, kids from underserved communities, inmates, and immigrant groups to teach them to start their own low- and no-cost press. There are organizations in many communities that provide creative writing workshops to these groups, and that's incredible, important work that could be amplified by giving the most avid learners in those groups access to the tools used to publish the poetry of their peers as PDFs and print-on-demand books, all at very little cost. It would be very powerful to pair the ethos of the mimeo movement in the 70s—where people were stealing time and resources at work to make poetry journals on the office Xerox machine—with an awareness of the need to provide a platform for marginalized voices.

But at a minimum, we can help each other survive whatever's coming through creative work, any form of making, and supporting the creative work of others in as many ways as possible. Host readings. Buy art if and when you can. Go to shows. Write reviews. Publish what you can. Be active. Stay engaged. These things are important. There is no clear line between art and politics. This is how we see and hear each other, and it's something we can all do better, in new ways that create more compelling interventions. That's always the goal.

ABOUT THE AUTHORS

MICHAEL FLATT is a PhD candidate in the Poetics Program at SUNY Buffalo. He was named by J. Michael Martinez to the Poetry Society of America's 2013 list of New American Poets for his book, *Absent Receiver* (SpringGun Press), and he is the founder of Low Frequency Press.

DERRICK MUND received his MFA in poetry from CU Boulder. He is the founder of the Leon Reading Series, and co-founder and board member of the Denver Small Press Festival. He works, edits, and teaches in Detroit Michigan.

ABOUT THE ARTIST: SUCHITRA MATTAI

Born in Guyana, South America, with Caribbean and South Asian heritage, I have had the opportunity to live in places such as Nova Scotia, Philadelphia, New York City, Minneapolis, France, and Udaipur, India. These diverse natural and cultural environments have greatly influenced my work and research. While my practice includes a wide range of materials and ideas, my primary focus is on the role of land and environment in the creation of identity. I create landscapes that incorporate cultural artifacts in an effort to subvert their original meanings. Through painting, drawing, collage, installation, video, and sculpture, I weave narratives of "the other," invoking fractured landscapes and reclaiming cultural artifacts (often colonial and domestic in nature).

I received an MFA in Painting and Drawing and an MA in South Asian art, both from the University of Pennsylvania, Philadelphia. I have exhibited my work in Philadelphia, New York City, Washington, DC, Minneapolis, Denver, Austin, Berlin, London, and Wales and my work has appeared in various publications such as The Daily Serving (Mailee Hung), New American Paintings, and will be in a forthcoming book, "A Collection of Contemporary Women's Voices on Guyana," (Grace Anezia Ali, Brill Press). Recent and upcoming projects include participation in an international biennial (2019), commissions with the Museum of Contemporary Art Denver and the Denver Art Museum, solo exhibitions at the Center for Visual Arts, Metropolitan State University of Denver, K Contemporary Art, and GrayDuck Gallery, as well as group exhibitions with the Center on Contemporary Art Seattle, RedLine Contemporary Art, and a travelling exhibition with the Museum of the Americas, Washington, DC. I am represented by K Contemporary Art Denver, and GrayDuck Gallery.

In my practice, land is a conceptual space for the exploration of identity. The places I create are born from memory, history and imagination. Land can offer sanctuary or peril, sometimes both simultaneously. Through installations, mixed media drawings and paintings, collages, and video, I explore how our natural environment(s) shapes personal narratives, ancestral histories and constructions of "self."

I want my work to be both intimate and vast. Landscape allows me a wide visual lens within which to situate intimate cultural artifacts and discuss the inextricably intertwined relationship of history and identity.

Combining fragments of landscape, vintage objects (often domestic), and culturally specific patterns, I create a nonlinear dialogue with the past. My current projects investigate the role of land in migrations, assimilations, and the creation of "home."

The work used for the cover of *Chlorosis* is "Ambiguity in the face of the cause," a 2016 piece made with thread on vintage needlepoint. It is from of a larger series of threadwork titled "Sublime Geometry."

In these works, I transform vintage needlepoints by embroidering a new layer of meaning onto the original pastoral (and distinctively European) scenes, which introduces an artificial element into the natural wooded landscapes. The interjections interrupt and complicate the original scape.

Learn more about the artist at
www.suchitramattai.com

WHY PRINT / DOCUMENT?

The Operating System uses the language "print document" to differentiate from the book-object as part of our mission to distinguish the act of documentation-in-book-FORM from the act of publishing as a backwards-facing replication of the book's agentive *role* as it may have appeared the last several centuries of its history. Ultimately, I approach the book as TECHNOLOGY: one of a variety of printed documents (in this case, bound) that humans have invented and in turn used to archive and disseminate ideas, beliefs, stories, and other evidence of production.

Ownership and use of printing presses and access to (or restriction of printed materials) has long been a site of struggle, related in many ways to revolutionary activity and the fight for civil rights and free speech all over the world. While (in many countries) the contemporary quotidian landscape has indeed drastically shifted in its access to platforms for sharing information and in the widespread ability to "publish" digitally, even with extremely limited resources, the importance of publication on physical media has not diminished. In fact, this may be the most critical time in recent history for activist groups, artists, and others to insist upon learning, establishing, and encouraging personal and community documentation practices. Hear me out.

With The OS's print endeavors I wanted to open up a conversation about this: the ultimately radical, transgressive act of creating PRINT /DOCUMENTATION in the digital age. It's a question of the archive, and of history: who gets to tell the story, and what evidence of our life, our behaviors, our experiences are we leaving behind? We can know little to nothing about the future into which we're leaving an unprecedentedly digital document trail — but we can be assured that publications, government agencies, museums, schools, and other institutional powers that be will continue to leave BOTH a digital and print version of their production for the official record. Will we?

As a (rogue) anthropologist and long time academic, I can easily pull up many accounts about how lives, behaviors, experiences — how THE STORY of a time or place — was pieced together using the deep study of correspondence, notebooks, and other physical documents which are no longer the norm in many lives and practices. As we move our creative behaviors towards digital note taking, and even audio and video, what can we predict about future technology that is in any way assuring that our stories will be accurately told – or told at all? How will we leave these things for the record?

In these documents we say:
WE WERE HERE, WE EXISTED, WE HAVE A DIFFERENT STORY

 - Lynne DeSilva-Johnson, Founder/Creative Director
THE OPERATING SYSTEM, Brooklyn NY 2018

RECENT & FORTHCOMING
OS PRINT / DOCUMENTS 2018-19

2019

Ark Hive-Marthe Reed
A Bony Framework for the Tangible Universe-D. Allen [kin(d)*]
Śnienie / Dreaming - Marta Zelwan/Krystyna Sakowicz, (Poland, trans. Victoria Miluch)
Opera on TV-James Brunton [kin(d)*]
Alparegho: Pareil-À-Rien / Alparegho, Like Nothing Else - Hélène Sanguinetti (France, trans. Ann Cefola)
Hall of Waters-Berry Grass [kin(d)*]
High Tide Of The Eyes - Bijan Elahi (Farsi-English/dual-language) trans. Rebecca Ruth Gould and Kayvan Tahmasebian
I Made for You a New Machine and All it Does is Hope - Richard Lucyshyn
Illusory Borders-Heidi Reszies
Transitional Object-Adrian Silbernagel [kin(d)*]
A Year of Misreading the Wildcats - Orchid Tierney
In the Drying Shed of Souls: Poetry from Cuba's Generation Zero Katherine Hedeen and Víctor Rodríguez Núñez, translators/editors
Street Gloss - Brent Armendinger with translations for Alejandro Méndez, Mercedes Roffé, Fabián Casas, Diana Bellessi, and Néstor Perlongher (Argentina)
Operation on a Malignant Body - Sergio Loo (Mexico, trans. Will Stockton)
Are There Copper Pipes in Heaven - Katrin Ottarsdóttir (Faroe Islands, trans. Matthew Landrum)

2018

An Absence So Great and Spontaneous It Is Evidence of Light - Anne Gorrick
The Book of Everyday Instruction - Chloë Bass
Executive Orders Vol. II - a collaboration with the Organism for Poetic Research
One More Revolution - Andrea Mazzariello
The Suitcase Tree - Filip Marinovich
Chlorosis - Michael Flatt and Derrick Mund
Sussuros a Mi Padre - Erick Sáenz
Sharing Plastic - Blake Nemec
The Book of Sounds - Mehdi Navid (Farsi dual language, trans. Tina Rahimi
In Corpore Sano : Creative Practice and the Challenged Body [Anthology]
Abandoners - Lesley Ann Wheeler
Jazzercise is a Language - Gabriel Ojeda-Sague
Return Trip / Viaje Al Regreso - Israel Dominguez; (Cuba, trans. Margaret Randall)
Born Again - Ivy Johnson
Attendance - Rocío Carlos and Rachel McLeod Kaminer
Singing for Nothing - Wally Swist
The Ways of the Monster - Jay Besemer
Walking Away From Explosions in Slow Motion - Gregory Crosby
Field Guide to Autobiography - Melissa Eleftherion
Kawsay: The Flame of the Jungle - María Vázquez Valdez (Mexico, trans. Margaret Randall)

2018 CHAPBOOK SERIES:

Want-catcher - Adra Raine; We, The Monstrous - Mark DuCharme;
Greater Grave - Jacq Greyja; Needles of Itching Feathers - Jared Schickling

DOC U MENT
/däkyəmənt/

First meant "instruction" or "evidence," whether written or not.

noun - a piece of written, printed, or electronic matter that provides information or evidence or that serves as an official record
verb - record (something) in written, photographic, or other form
synonyms - paper - deed - record - writing - act - instrument

[Middle English, precept, from Old French, from Latin *documentum*, example, proof, from *docre*, to teach; see *dek-* in Indo-European roots.]

Who is responsible for the manufacture of value?

Based on what supercilious ontology have we landed in a space where we vie against other creative people in vain pursuit of the fleeting credibilities of the scarcity economy, rather than freely collaborating and sharing openly with each other in ecstatic celebration of MAKING?

While we understand and acknowledge the economic pressures and fear-mongering that threatens to dominate and crush the creative impulse, we also believe that **now more than ever we have the tools to relinquish agency via cooperative means,** fueled by the fires of the Open Source Movement.

Looking out across the invisible vistas of that rhizomatic parallel country we can begin to see our community beyond constraints, in the place where intention meets resilient, proactive, collaborative organization.

Here is a document born of that belief, sown purely of imagination and will. When we document we assert. We print to make real, to reify our being there. When we do so with mindful intention to address our process, to open our work to others, to create beauty in words in space, to respect and acknowledge the strength of the page we now hold physical, a thing in our hand, we remind ourselves that, like Dorothy: *we had the power all along, my dears.*

THE PRINT! DOCUMENT SERIES

is a project of
the trouble with bartleby
in collaboration with
the operating system

www.ingramcontent.com/pod-product-compliance
Lightning Source LLC
Chambersburg PA
CBHW020124130526
44591CB00032B/520